VISION IN VISIBILITY

The Silent Generation Speaks

Patricia A. Terrangi

Vision in Visibility: The Silent Generation Speaks

Published by Bell-Boyd Publishing

P.O. Box 15142 Chesapeake VA 23328

Cover design by Wisdom and Legacy Consulting, LLC

Manufactured in the United States of America
Paperback ISBN: 979-8-9932145-3-5
Hardcover ISBN: 979-8-9932145-4-2

DEDICATION

To God be the Glory!

I dedicate this book to the Holy Spirit, who inspired the vision and content of this work in my spirit. I am forever grateful for His guidance, wisdom, and strategies shared with me throughout every stage of this journey.

Thank You for being my Teacher, my Revealer, and my Constant Companion—speaking in moments of silence, bringing clarity in times of uncertainty, and giving me the courage to write what could not be seen. You illuminated what was hidden and gave language to what was once unspoken.

This work is a reflection of Your presence, Your power, and Your voice. May every page carry Your truth, and may every reader encounter Your love, be awakened to their invisibility and find the confidence to be seen, heard, and known in this season of their lives.

Finally, Thank You for choosing me to speak on behalf of the invisible generation. What was birthed in the spirit, I now release for Your glory.

In the name of Jesus, Amen.

ACKNOWLEDGMENTS

To the memory of my mother, Barbara S. Rucker, who taught me what strength looks like when it is wrapped in gentleness --- thank you. I thank God for the time we shared together.

In memory of my husband and friend, Andre Terrangi—you are missed. I am sorry that the health care you needed came too late.

My beloved children, Terrell, Tara, Tonya, and my son in love Mike, thank you for being a pillar of strength, encouragement, and love as I move forward in this season of my life. I thank God for you and your loving kindness.

To my amazing grandchildren, Taj, Tia, Teyuana, my grandson in love Carlos, and my great-grandchildren, you are my greater joy and the continuation of our family legacy, which lives on through you.

To Coach Jackie B. Grice, my dear friend, from the very first time I shared with you, that I had an assignment from God to write this book, her enthusiasm, insightful suggestions, prayers, and unwavering support have been truly indispensable during this journey. Thank you.

To Pastor A. Deaneen Goodrich, my mentor and dear friend, I am grateful for you. Thank you for the strategic, purposeful, and powerful prayers that covered me and prophetic words of wisdom spoken into me during this assignment from God.

To my dear friend Lawanda Artis, I am grateful for every word of encouragement, every prayer, and always your support. Thank you.

To my dear friend Wendy Hobbs, I appreciate every word of encouragement and your assistance in gathering information.

To Bishop K. W. and Dr. Elder V.K. Brown, I am forever grateful for over twenty years of your Kingdom leadership, spiritual covering, and empowering preaching and teaching. Your dedication to God, Kingdom principles, love for others, and your global perspective have greatly impacted my life as I live for Christ. I graciously thank you.

To Pastor James (LJAY) Brown and First Lady Dr. Keshia, your inspiring teaching strengthened and encouraged my heart. Thank you.

Thank you, Dr. Angela Corprew-Boyd. I am indebted to you for helping me to manifest the assignment given to me by the Holy Spirit. I appreciate your openness to innovative ideas and new perspectives, commitment to accountability, and sharing a desire to always please God with all that is done.

To every older adult who shared their stories, wisdom and experiences that are shared in this book, though in most cases names were changed, you are recognized and appreciated. Your voices are no longer silent as you become more visible.

To younger generations dedicated to meaningful conversations with older adults, sharing wisdom and experiences for lasting change across generations. Thank you.

To every family member, friend, and professional liaison, I am grateful to you for your encouraging words and support. Thank you.

To everyone who has taken the time to read *Vision in Visibility*, I am immensely grateful. It is my prayer that we become better in our relationships with one another, especially older adults. You and I must commit to supporting change agents, health care related, socially, politically, in our communities and states to impact outdated mindsets and practices. We, too, must commit to being agents of change. Aging should not merely be viewed as the passage of time. It is God's blessing upon our lives and a continuation to our story.

Thank you for staying with me to the end.

CONTENTS

FORWARD

Jackie B. Grice

There was a season in my life when I sat under a tree for two days in silence.

No phone.

No agenda.

No speaking.

Just stillness.

I was not trying to make a statement. I was trying to listen. And what I learned in that silence is that what goes unnoticed is not always unimportant. Sometimes it is simply unseen.

That is why I said yes to writing this foreword.

Patricia Terrangi is not just an author to me. She is a dear friend. A woman I have coached. A woman I have watched wrestle honestly with questions about aging, purpose, visibility, and voice. When she told me what this book would confront — the quiet invisibility that can accompany aging — I knew this was not a casual project. It was necessary.

We live in a culture that moves fast. Faster every year. Youth is marketed. Innovation is celebrated. Reinvention is applauded. And somewhere along the way, aging became something to manage instead of something to honor. This book gently — but firmly — challenges that shift.

It asks hard questions.

When did we start assuming older adults have less to contribute?

When did wisdom become "outdated"?

When did experience begin to feel like excess baggage?

Through personal reflections and stories, Patricia opens space for older adults to name what they have felt but may not have voiced: moments of being overlooked, dismissed, or quietly sidelined. She also speaks about loneliness without dramatizing it, about health without shaming it, and about advocacy without anger. One image she shares — three chairs secured together at different heights — stayed with me. She sees the generations connected, dependent on one another. If the clasps loosen, the structure weakens. That metaphor is not dramatic. It is accurate. We need each other.

Older adults are not a separate category of society; they are the continuation of it. They carry memory. They carry history. They carry lessons we have not yet lived long enough to understand. This book also recognizes caregivers — those who walk alongside aging parents and loved ones — and even includes a husband and wife who navigated that journey together. It acknowledges the tenderness and the fatigue. The devotion and the strain. It does not romanticize caregiving, but it respects it.

What I appreciate most about Patricia's approach is that she does not end with a complaint. She ends with responsibility. She invites older adults to reset their thinking. To steward their health. To mentor. To pray. To continue growing. She challenges readers to confront ageism in practical ways — from everyday jokes to systemic discrimination. And she anchors the entire message in scripture and hope. Visibility is not simply about being seen in a room.

It is about being valued in a room.

It is about being heard in a room.

It is about being remembered when decisions are made.

I agreed to write this foreword because I believe this conversation matters. I believe generational bridges matter. I believe voices that have grown quieter deserve to be amplified again. And I believe that aging is not a diminishing. It is a deepening.

As you read this book, I encourage you to sit with it. Let it confront you gently. Let it expand your thinking. Let it soften assumptions you may not have realized you carried.

There is vision in visibility. And when we choose to see differently, we live differently.

THE VISION

There are many stories that are shared with you in this book. The very first story is how the vision for this book originated.

I was awakened and prompted to get out of bed in the early morning about two years ago to pray or so I thought. Although I did not know how the Holy Spirit would lead me in this moment, I immediately thought about my aunt who was critically ill, and that I was awakened to pray for her. Relocating to another room, sitting down with my notebook and pen, I waited. Suddenly, my hand began to write and did not stop until the Holy Spirit had downloaded into me information to write a book about the invisibility of older adults in our society, and had provided me with content for each chapter.

I thank God for blessing me to write this book during this season of my life as an older adult. Now may you be blessed in every area of your life as you read and mediate on each chapter.

INTRODUCTION

Just for a moment imagine standing before a mirror that does not only reflect features, wrinkles, or gray hairs, but reveals how the world perceives you. For many older women, this mirror is not their own; it is, in fact, the mirror of society. As the years pass, the reflection grows more faded, less distinct, and all too often, begins to disappear. This is the mirror society holds up to its aging adults, and its reflection tells a story of growing invisibility.

What a way to begin to talk about how society contributes to the invisibility of older adults. This book begins with that image: an older woman gazing into a mirror, watching herself age. Yet, as she peers into the glass, she notices something unsettling. The world on the other side seems to turn away, as though she has slipped from view. Her life, experience, and wisdom blur as society's focus shifts elsewhere as though her value has expired with the passing years. You and I, the older adult, may have experienced at times that feeling of invisibility in our homes, communities, workplaces, media, and job market to name a few. To the older adult, situations such as these may contribute to a feeling of being unseen and unnoticed.

Yet the story does not end with fading away into invisibility. The mirror, as much as it reflects society's biases, also reveals opportunities for change. As older adults, you and I have the ability to challenge and transform societal perceptions that overlook our contributions and worth. It is timeout for those who retire, with no vision and no plan, for their lives. We must discontinue that mindset as we continue to learn, engage, and assert our perspectives for a more fulfilling lifestyle. By shifting how we view our lives, it is vital to focus on our vision the future. One of the ways we do so is by supporting, connecting, and actively building relationships across different age groups. Building bridges through intergenerational initiatives is a focal point. It builds up and strengthens the younger generations as they are exposed to the wisdom and experience of the older generations. It enables the older generation to develop greater proficiency in navigating new environments and adapting more efficiently.

Through personal stories and practical strategies, this book seeks to illuminate how older adults—especially women—can work around the societal mirror, polishing its surface until it accurately reflects their worth. It is a call to recognize, value, and celebrate the enduring contributions of all who have lived long enough to see their own reflection begin to blur, and to ensure that, instead, they shine. No matter where you are in the aging process, I challenge you to take an inventory of it. Ask yourself, is this where I desire to be at this season of my life. Then decide to become the person that the mirror cannot erase. There are many older adults who have been challenging society's misconceptions of what it is like to grow older. Some stories in this book will touch upon your life, vision, strength, endurance, and how you have been successful. This book is to remind you that we, the older adults, must refrain from giving more attention to how others see us than how we see ourselves. Rather, we can be grateful for and appreciate who we are today based on all the years and experiences it took to get here. You and I must allow our light to shine and continue to carry God's vision for us in our hearts as we move forward in it. Instead of focusing on society's reflection in the mirror of older adults, we must trust God and His promises for us as older adults. "For we walk by faith, not by sight" (2 Corinthians 5:7 NKJV).

I hope this book touches your heart and spirit as deeply as the journey of writing it has touched mine. My prayer for you is that, as you look into the mirror each day, you begin to see a powerful, seasoned older adult who has lived, endured, laughed, and learned. We can rise above the narrow lens that society often places on us ---especially older women---and reclaim the fullness of who we were created to be. This book may not speak to every experience of aging, but I believe it holds nuggets of truth that can help reshape how you see yourself – as an older and wiser person whose life has meaning, purpose, and power just as God intended for you!

Provided for you, at the end of each chapter, are reflective questions that will navigate you to the truth of who you are and how your purpose in this season as an older adult is still impactful. Write your responses in the accompanying, My Reflective Journal, and continue to view yourself in the mirror to see the transformation.

Chapter 1

THE FEELING OF FADING AWAY

"Do not cast me away when I am old; do not forsake me when my strength is gone."
Psalm 71:9, NKJV

I once thought I understood the aging process—at least, better than most. For nearly two decades, I cared for my mother as she aged gracefully in my home. I witnessed firsthand the slow, quiet shifts that came with time. I remember vividly the day she said, with a mix of frustration and surrender, "I need you to take over my medicines and the bills." And another day, just as quietly, she handed over her car keys and never drove again.

Simple things—things she once did without thinking—became overwhelming for her. What used to be routine became stress-inducing. That is when I realized: aging is not simply about the physical body growing older. It is about the gradual shedding of independence, the quiet withdrawal from what was once familiar.

As I watched my mother retreat from social settings, I noticed her shrinking—not in body, but in spirit. She was becoming invisible.

And now, all these years later, I find myself standing in that same space.

I am now the oldest one in many rooms—whether I am at family gatherings, sitting in a doctor's office, out shopping, or participating in organizations I once helped to build. The shift is subtle but profound. Sometimes people talk around me instead of to me. Other times, my input is bypassed—as though age has made me obsolete.

Not long ago, I was invited to sit on an interview panel by an entrepreneurial friend. During the interview, the young man we were evaluating made direct eye contact with everyone on the panel—except me. Even when I asked him questions, he barely looked in my direction. I was the oldest at the table, and I felt invisible.

That is the emotional weight of aging that no one prepares you for. The feeling that you are slowly fading into the background. You are no longer the main character in your own life story. It is not always intentional, but it is deeply felt. Have you felt it too? Have you ever watched someone you love go through this experience—or perhaps you are in the middle of it yourself? The quiet ache of invisibility? The subtle shift in how the world perceives you, listens to you, or fails to acknowledge you altogether?

In many Eastern cultures, aging is revered. Elders are held in high esteem. The Bible reminds us in Job 12:12, NKJV, "Wisdom is with the aged, and understanding in length of days." Still, in Western society, we often view aging as something to hide or fear.

The term "ageism" was coined by psychiatrist and gerontologist Dr. Robert Butler in 1969. He defined it as "a systematic process of stereotyping and discrimination against people simply because they are old."[1]

As a society, we are youth-obsessed. We glorify the young, airbrush the signs of age, and too often dismiss the voices of our elders; but aging is not a disease. It is a divine process. And though our strength may change, our value should never diminish.

If you are over 65, perhaps you have already recognized these quiet moments of invisibility. They come in different forms—being overlooked in conversations, dismissed in decisions, or simply no longer being invited to the table where you once led. But let me be clear: We are not invisible. We are powerful.

We carry the weight of generations. We have lived through joys, losses, miracles, and mistakes. We have knowledge that cannot be Googled and wisdom that cannot be bought.

There is an African proverb that says, "Those who respect the elderly pave their own road toward success." It is time we remind the world—and perhaps even remind ourselves—that we are not fading. We are rising into a new season, and we have every right to be seen, heard, and honored.

In the chapters to come, we will explore what it means to live well and fully as we age—with intention, dignity, and grace. We will talk about health, relationships, money, and legacy. But before we go any further, I ask you to do this:

Look in the mirror.

See yourself—fully.

And know, you are still here.

Write your thoughts down in your *Reflective Journal*. Share them with someone you trust or say them aloud in prayer. Your voice deserves to be heard—even if only by you and God.

1. When was the first time you felt overlooked or unseen because of your age?

2. How did it make you feel—and how did you respond?

3. Are there areas in your life where you have started to retreat or withdraw?

4. What would it look like for you to reclaim those spaces?

5. What should you be ready to remind yourself of based on your life story when you feel invisible?

Chapter 2

RE-EXAMINE AND RESET

"As a man thinketh in his heart, so is he."
Proverbs 23:7, NKJV

The reflection we see as society metaphorically holds the mirror up to our faces, the older person, emphasizes the years passing as we age. The fallacy is that it does not reveal the wisdom- rich experiences gained, community lifestyle, professional life, healthcare access, educational gains, spirituality, and various relationships. Aging is not just about adding years – it is about unlearning, reexamining, and resetting how we define ourselves.

When I look in the mirror, I see fine lines, yes—but I also see stories. I see a woman who has loved, led, laughed, and survived things nobody ever trained her to expect. I see a mother, grandmother and great-grandmother among my many blessed roles in life. I see someone who is an encourager, who has comforted others, and someone who could follow as well as lead in life. I see someone who has a God given plan for her life. When you look in the mirror, you should see that God has a plan for you too.

We are blessed to be a part of life's journey. We have been entrusted with this gift. People are living longer than ever before. Healthier, too—if we are intentional about it. Our ancestors did not always have the privilege of imagining life past 60. They worked until their bodies gave out. They raised families, carried grief in silence, and too often died before being celebrated. So let me say this to you, if you are alive, aging, and reading this—you are already a miracle.

Society, as it stands today, is still playing catch-up. It does not quite know what to do with all this vibrant longevity. In our culture, youthfulness is idolized while in Eastern cultures, the older population is highly revered, given much honor, and rewarded in different ways for their wisdom and experience.

Still, there is a shift. A slow, powerful shift. A study done by AARP in 2024 revealed that society was beginning to be more receptive of the contributions of older women and men. The Baby Boomers, born between 1946 and 1964, are rewriting the narrative for the lifestyle of the older population. As older women, we are not sitting quietly on porches with crocheted blankets unless we want to be. Our age group is starting businesses, getting degrees, mentoring young people, running marathons, and writing books. We are reclaiming space and resetting our lives for better days ahead.

Let us talk about those quiet moments that creep up on you. The first time a stranger calls you "dear" or "young lady" with a tone that suggests anything but youth. I remember being at a grocery store, just trying to buy my greens and black-eyed peas.

The young woman at the register smiled sweetly and said, "Let me help you, dear."

Now listen, I know she meant well—but it was like someone switched the lights on in my head. Oh, I thought, we are here now. I am the "dear." Then there is that moment when our own children start speaking to us in that slowed-down voice. You know the one. The one they used with their grandmother. A voice laced with good intentions but dripping with the assumption that we are fragile or confused. I raised those babies. Changed their diapers, nursed them through heartbreaks, taught them how to drive. And now they want to explain the remote control to me like I did not teach them how to use one.

That is when it hits you—not like a thunderclap, but like a gentle rain: the roles are shifting. We have moved from center stage to the supporting cast. From mother to matriarch. From worker bee to wisdom-keeper.

But here is where the power lies. In this season of life, we get to reclaim and redefine who we are. In 2 Corinthians 12:9, NKJV, the Word tells us that "God's grace is sufficient for us, and that our strength is made perfect in weakness." How can we not be encouraged and activated to move forward with our lives as we share the goodness of the Lord with others? Life is too precious for us to retreat when things get tough in any area of our lives. We must challenge the stereotypes connected with getting older. There are many barriers we face as we get older, so we should not give in to thoughts of removing ourselves from living the best life possible right where we are.

In her book, *Disrupt Aging*, former AARP CEO Jo Ann Jenkins stated: "Our perceptions about aging are out of sync with our reality."[2] She challenges us to see aging as the opening of new doors—new ideas, new passions, and new adventures. I could not agree more.

That is why I call this chapter "Re-examine and Reset." We must examine again not just how the world sees us, but how we see ourselves. What dreams have you put on hold because you thought the time had passed? Stop believing the hype of society that your best days are behind you.

There is still time to write that book. To start that business. To learn to swim. To take that solo trip. To speak your truth at a family gathering. To laugh loudly without apology. You are the sum of every sacrifice, every prayer whispered in the dark, every "yes" and "no" you have ever spoken. You are a living archive of stories this world desperately needs. You are a spiritual compass for your family and community. And more than anything, you are still becoming. Therefore, reset because you are not a burden, but you are still evolving.

I hope the following reflective questions will spark a new flame in the fire of your way of thinking about who you are and where you dare to dream, and follow through on living today your best life.

Write your thoughts down in your *Reflective Journal*. Share them with someone you trust or say them aloud in prayer. Your voice deserves to be heard—even if only by you and God.

1. What beliefs about aging did you inherit from your family or community? Are those beliefs still serving you today?

2. Can you identify a recent moment where you felt "invisible?" How did it make you feel—and how might you reclaim your space?

3. In what ways have your roles changed over time, and how have you adjusted emotionally and spiritually?

4. What is one dream or goal you thought was "too late" to pursue—but still whispers to you today?

5. How can you begin to "reset" your perspective and lifestyle to align with your current values and truth?

Chapter 3

TIME FOR A MINDSET SHIFT: HOW DO WE GET FROM HERE TO THERE

"For everything there is a season, a time for every activity under heaven."
Ecclesiastes 3:1, NLT

Is it a compliment or not when someone tells you that you look good for your age? Have you ever been told at a job interview that you would be bored with the job? What about being told you should act your age? Yes, these questions may very well deal with ageism. As addressed in a previous chapter, ageism refers to discrimination directed toward an individual based on their age. It impacts people of all ages.

Have you or someone you know wrestled with turning 50, 60, or 70? What is the reason for this? Is it fear, and if so what is causing it? Stop listening to the old cliques that say to you that you have nothing to contribute, or you are too old. Sometimes rather than enjoy the age we are blessed to be, we began to get silent about our age. When I reached my 60's, I remember being in groups of people when the subject on age would come up, and I just got silent.

Now listen, do not judge me. I am not alone in this. Some of you may have done the same thing. You and I cannot ignore the truth that we are getting older. It is a natural process of living. However, neither should we be required to adopt society's typical perspective or behavior toward older adults. You and I are not invisible. If we believe that we are a new creation in Christ, then let us ask God to use us in new ways as He transforms our thinking. We cannot overlook or try to laugh off ageist messages as they show up in our everyday lives. Remember those birthday cards that refer to being "over the hill," as if growing older is not a normal process of living. Or the times in which we may be overlooked or ignored even though we are next in line to be served. Or what about the medical visits where our concerns are seemingly taken lightly, and we are told "That is just part of getting old." These messages are not necessarily subtle and certainly not harmless. They reinforce a society that diminishes our worth as older adults rather than honor our wisdom, experiences and contributions.

Both you and I have the capacity and responsibility to actively pursue and facilitate the changes that are necessary and desired. One way to meet this challenge and become more empowered is through supporting various organizations dedicated to enhancing the quality of life as we age. One of the most respected and impactful national and well-known organization is the American Association of Retired Persons known today as AARP for anyone 50 years old and over. AARP and similar organizations advance this goal by advocating, providing resources, and providing community programs that emphasize the contributions of older adults.

Examining the shift from invisibility to visibility for older adults prompts us to reflect on our societal values and their evolution. In Aging Sideways: Changing Our Perspectives on Getting Older (2024), gerontologist Jeanette Leardi notes that ageism, whether conscious or unconscious, can make older adults feel invisible. She also notes that because people in our age group are often overlooked, society fails to acknowledge the value of our skills and experience.[3]

Yet, as we reframe our thinking towards growing older, we must be able to emphasize this is not just a challenge for the older population. Instead, we must view this from an interdisciplinary team perspective to bring about lasting change. This involves intentional, yet spontaneous, communication and interaction between families, communities, and various agencies. Some of the challenges we face, as older adults, may be caused by loss in our lives – a loved one, a career, downsizing, relocation, medical issues, and finances. Many older adults have a plan for these times, but some do not. If our families are not our support group, then we may need to seek support elsewhere. This can be problematic depending upon physical health, social and emotional health, and finances. Some agencies of this nature, however, will be provided in a resource list at the end of the book.

We recognize that individual life circumstances vary, and that issues concerning one older person does not necessarily concern another. You and I may not experience the same challenges in our communities, health, finances, education, relationships, faith- based connections, and other community support. However, because we are living in an ageist society, it benefits us and those around us to focus on reframing ageism. This requires a mindset shift to create positive change for our personal lives, homes, families, professions, and communities. We, as older adults, play a key role in shaping societal perceptions of ageism through our conduct, communication, and daily interactions, as well as by supporting organizations, community groups, and faith-based ministries. We are blessed to grow older and to be able to challenge ourselves and others to change how aging is viewed in society.

According to former AARP CEO and author Jo Ann Jenkins in her book on *Disrupt Aging*, she gives two reasons for not accepting ageism in our society. "First, ageism - and the negative perception of aging that it perpetuates – creates a negative reality of aging. And, as long as that exists, we will never face up to the changes we need to make to adapt to our aging society. Second, it is bad enough that ageism can influence public policy, employment practices, and how people are treated in society, but what is worst is that we accept the ageist behavior ourselves and start acting it out."[4]

We must begin to reframe our way of thinking about how we believe in the aging process. Have you asked yourself or asked others, "What does the aging process mean to you? Most of us have heard the phrase "act your age" whether it was spoken to us or whether we spoke it to others. As a parent, we may have spoken it to our children "act your age." But what does it say to you as an older adult if someone tells you to "act your age." Could it be that person was thinking "act your "older" age?" Is this viewed as ageist language? We do not tell our children or grandchildren to "act your "younger" age." Despite shared backgrounds and experiences, we remain unique older adults with plenty to contribute to our families, communities, workplaces, churches, and other social groups while we are successfully aging. Let us stop emphasizing the limitations society may place on us because of age, and agree to focus on the actions and behaviors leading to new ways of living our lives no matter what age we may be. Let us work collaboratively to challenge outdated perceptions and foster a society where aging is regarded with respect and dignity. "For with God, nothing shall be impossible," (Luke 1:37, NKJV).

Write your thoughts down in your *Reflective Journal.* Share them with someone you trust or say them aloud in prayer. Your voice deserves to be heard—even if only by you and God.

1. Take a moment to think about some beliefs you hold about aging that may need to shift.
2. How can you help change ageist attitudes and behaviors toward yourself and others?
3. When were some of those times you were told you were either "too young" or "too old" to do something in your life that you felt was important to you? How did that make you feel?
4. Who in your life needs to hear that they still have value – no matter their age?
5. What role has faith or spirituality played in how you view your own aging process?

Chapter 4

SEE ME FOR ME: UNMASKING THE LONELINESS

"He heals the brokenhearted and binds up their wounds."
Psalm 147:3, NIV

Loneliness and isolation are intermingled in our experiences of invisibility. When you and I as older adults are not recognized as valued or connected members of society, we may begin to feel overlooked, leading to loneliness or isolation.

When I was in the process of starting to write this chapter, I shared with a very wise person in my life how I was seeking God on how it was to be shaped. It was a difficult chapter for me to write. The next day, during church, my Pastor delivered a sermon called "Provision in a Season of Exhaustion," (1 Kings 19:1-8), which reassured me that I should continue writing even when facing delays, setbacks, silence, pain, and uncertainty. It was the second point in my Pastor's message entitled "Loneliness of the Journey" that the prophet Elijah perceived he was facing that convicted and encouraged me. Elijah perceived that he was alone after a great victory over his enemies. This resulted in his depression, isolation, and eventual loneliness. In various circumstances, you and I may have experienced exhaustion, loneliness, and isolation in our lives after successful life events that occur as we grow older. Our family status and dynamics, our health, our communities, our finances, and other relationships change. Loneliness may enter our lives through loss of loved ones, retirement, health challenges, or relocations. Although robust support systems are necessary in such situations, they may not always be available to older adults.

Being apart from family and loved ones during the holidays can lead to feelings of loneliness and isolation. A friend of mine shared that she had not put up a Christmas tree in her home for the past three years during the holidays because she did not expect anyone to come to her home. She noted that she was not home on Christmas day. Is this the type of behavior that leads to loneliness and social isolation? This might indeed be the case. Loneliness affects people of all ages - the young and the old, married and single, women and men. No one really escapes this emotion, and many experience it on a frequent basis. Have you ever been in a room full of people and still felt lonely? God created us to be in relationship with one another. This seems to become more difficult, but not impossible, for older adults. Although maintaining social connections may present greater challenges with age, they remain essential for overall well-being and a fulfilling life.

Many of us have lived full lives and desire to continue to do so as we age. Older adults are more adversely affected by loneliness. To effectively address loneliness and isolation, it is essential to proactively foster social connections and maintain meaningful relationships with family, friends, colleagues, communities, organizations, faith-based institutions, healthcare providers, and society at large, even in circumstances where one's efforts may not be immediately recognized by others and even when we feel invisible. Loneliness and isolation can make older adults feel even more invisible. When we talk about loneliness, it is difficult not to recall the COVID Pandemic in 2021. We were confined in our homes, with very restrictive movement. This was a time of uncertainty, isolation, and loneliness for everyone, especially for the aging population.

Loneliness is more than being socially isolated. Loneliness is "the distressing feeling of being alone or separated. Social isolation is the lack of social contacts and having few people to interact with regularly."[5] Our age group does not experience the highest rate of loneliness. People aged 18–34 experience loneliness and social isolation more than any other age group. However, more than one third of people aged 50 to 80 feel lonely. In May 2023, the U.S. Surgeon General, Vivek Murthy, called loneliness a public health epidemic while an APA Poll in 2024 at a minimum once a week found that 30% of adults reported experiencing loneliness.[6]

The world operates at an increasingly rapid pace due to advances in technology and immediate access to information. While some suggest this could alleviate loneliness among boomers, it does not serve as a substitute for in-person relationships and interactions. In many cases, the older adult may be left behind in this area. Many of us as older adults have a schedule that keeps us active. We talk with our children daily and friends too. We attend church on a regular basis and volunteer to serve. Many people actively participate in their community by volunteering and joining local groups. Someone might wonder, then why do we feel lonely? Loneliness is not just about being isolated or secluded from others. It concerns the perception of our current position in relation to where we believe we should be. Most people have felt lonely at some point.

Experiencing loneliness is not the same for all people because people are different. We understand that living meaningful lifestyles is not the same for every older person. Moving to a new location, experiencing the loss of friends or family, retiring, or undergoing notable changes in physical health can lead to feelings of loneliness. When we move to a new location, we leave behind the familiar – family and friends, special places we have learned to love. Before I retired, I moved eight times with the same organization. Even though this was good for my career, it did cause at times loneliness and isolation, especially when it separated me from my family. We can probably testify that the lack of meaningful social connections can heighten the sense of being invisible in society.

When loneliness leads to anxiety and depression, it can lead to negative consequences on the physical body. In response to this widespread issue, certain countries have adopted policies whereby older adults are placed with younger family households instead of living independently. Dr. Joe Coughlin, Director and Founder of the Massachusetts Institute of Technology Age Lab, stated "People are preparing for wealth, and they are preparing for death, but those are bookends. There are many chapters in between...if you do not have a place to go, people to be with, or things to do, that is not a complete life."[7]

Some of the stories shared with me on this matter, I want to share with you. While you may or may not see yourself in them, you may recognize someone you know - a family member, a friend, or a neighbor. Ask yourself, what can I do to change how I think and act in similar situations, and what role do I have to affect situations like these? Remember, the change has to start with each one of us.

Three Aging Scenarios

Scenario 1

Your aging friend and neighbor, who lives alone, has recently begun refusing visits. For several weeks she has not answered the door, nor has she returned phone calls – a marked departure from her usual behavior. Other neighbors have noticed the change as well, and concern is growing. This sudden withdrawal may signal loneliness, depression, or the quiet weight of isolation. Eventually, you connect with one of her relatives, who shares that she is deeply afraid of growing old alone. With this understanding, the question becomes clear: how can you offer meaningful support during this vulnerable season?

Scenario 2

You felt a surge of excitement when your adult children invited you to lunch. Yet as you sit across from them in the restaurant, surrounded by the low hum of conversation and clinking dishes, an unexpected loneliness settles in. Their attention remains fixed on their cell phones, and meaningful conversation never quite begins. In the midst of the crowd, you begin to feel unseen – wondering whether they truly notice your presence or if you have somehow become invisible to them. The moment raises a quiet but piercing question: how do you respond when people you love most are physically present, yet emotionally distant?

Scenario 3

During a workplace meeting, you find yourself the most experienced professional in the room – and the only older adult among younger peers. You offer thoughtful strategies aligned with the goals set by leadership, yet your contributions seem to pass unnoticed, met with silence or quickly overshadowed. The experience feels uncomfortably familiar. When insight born in years of practice is overlooked, it raises an unsettling question: Does being the oldest in the room diminish your perceived value? And in moments like these, how easy is it to begin doubting your relevance to the team?

Write your thoughts down in your *Reflective Journal*. Share them with someone you trust or say them aloud in prayer. Your voice deserves to be heard—even if only by you and God.

1. Think about your support systems for a moment. Describe and write about how you are valued by them.
2. When was the most recent time that you engaged in social activities in your family, community, or faith-based organizations? Do you feel connected in these moments?
3. If you do not engage, what will it take for you to become involved?
4. What is it that brings you joy?
5. Which of the situations above do you relate to most? Why?

Chapter 5

A JOURNEY OF COMPASSION AND SUPPORT: UNNOTICED, INVISIBLE, YET SO INVALUABLE

"All praise to God, the Father of our Lord Jesus Christ. God is our merciful Father and the source of all comfort. He comforts us in all our troubles, so that we can comfort others..."
2 Corinthians 1:3–4, NLT

As we reflect on what it means to become "invisible" as we age, it is important to recognize how easily older adults step into caregiving roles—sometimes by choice, and sometimes simply because there is no one else. At this stage of life, we may find ourselves caring for a spouse, a sibling, an adult child, a close friend, or even a neighbor. Today, a caregiver is often described simply as someone responsible for the care of another— but that description barely scratches the surface of the emotional, spiritual, and physical weight the role truly carries.

Many of the plans we once made for our later years, travel, church service, or simply enjoying quiet days, are often placed on hold when caregiving becomes necessary. And caregiving does not belong to one age group. We care for our children when they are young. We care for our parents as they age. We care for friends and family when illness or hardship appears. In truth, caregiving is a lifelong calling that moves in seasons. Former First Lady Rosalynn Carter once said, "There are only four kinds of people in the world: those who have been caregivers, those who are currently caregivers, those who will be caregivers, and those who will need caregivers."[8] With age, I have come to believe that this is not simply an observation—it is a promise of shared humanity. At some point, every one of us will stand in one of those places.

As a mother, grandmother, great-grandmother, and yes, a widow for twenty-eight years, I have learned that life has a way of placing us on both sides of the caregiving journey. I have been the one who gave care, and I have also been the one who needed it. Both experiences have shaped me deeply. They taught me that love, when joined with compassion, often requires sacrifice—quiet sacrifice. It asks us to lay down parts of our own plans, our independence, and sometimes our sense of self, for the sake of someone we love.

I know what it is to set my own life aside to care for my husband, then my mother, and most recently my daughter. I also know the humility of seeing my family set aside their lives to care for me. Neither role is easy. And I suspect many of you reading this have lived some version of this story yourselves or have watched it unfold in the life of someone you love.

When caregiving enters our lives, our focus naturally shifts. We stop centering ourselves and turn our attention toward those entrusted to our care. We become supporters, intercessors, and quiet guardians of dignity. We pray more. We worry more. We love more. And we do our best to keep our loved ones comfortable as they heal, decline, or prepare for transition.

Caregiving is born out of love and sustained by compassion. Sometimes it is temporary. Sometimes it lasts years. Sometimes we step into it knowingly. Other times it arrives without warning. But no matter how it comes, compassion is the foundation. Scripture reminds us that God comforts us in our troubles so that we might comfort others. In that way, caregiving becomes an extension of God's mercy moving through human hands.

Yet caregivers often go unseen. Our work happens quietly, behind closed doors, away from applause or recognition. Society's attention remains fixed on the one receiving care—and rightly so—but the caregiver can slowly fade into the background. We become invisible, even as we carry heavy responsibility. Still, invisibility does not erase need.

I am reminded of the instructions given on an airplane before takeoff. The flight attendant points to the oxygen mask and tells us that in an emergency, we must put the mask on ourselves first before helping anyone else. That lesson applies to caregiving as well. If we neglect our own well-being—physically, emotionally, spiritually—we risk exhaustion, resentment, illness, and burnout. Stress can take many forms, including financial strain, emotional fatigue, and declining health. This is not a call to abandon responsibility. It is a call to wisdom.

Caregivers must learn to ask for help—from family, friends, church communities, and professionals. We must learn to set boundaries, even when it feels uncomfortable. We must make space for silence, prayer, reading, and resting in God's Word. There is no guilt in caring for yourself. In fact, caring for yourself is an act of stewardship.

We should recognize and express appreciation for the contributions of all caregivers—whether professionals, family members, or friends. However, this chapter focuses specifically on older adults who share their personal experiences as family caregivers. A 2025 study conducted by AARP and the National Alliance for Caregiving found that 63 million family caregivers navigate the shared challenges, stresses, and rewards of this role.[9] Caregiving affects individuals across many dimensions, including emotional, physical, financial, social, spiritual, and professional well-being. For this reason, self-care is essential for caregivers, who also need support and attention. Practicing self-care is not an act of selfishness, but a necessary way to maintain balance and sustain the ability to care well for others.

Before closing this chapter, I will share three caregiving stories—real lives, real sacrifices, real faith. If you are a caregiver, I encourage you to consider writing your own story. Putting words to your experience can be healing. It can help you see your journey with new clarity and discover strategies that nurture both the one you care for and yourself.

Caregiver Angela – I Can Still Do It Myself

I can still remember the sound I assumed was a book falling to the floor in my Ma's bedroom. Instead, it was her tray table, its contents scattered across the floor. By the time I reached the back bedroom—down what felt like a mile-long hallway—I found my 85-year-old mother on her knees, carefully gathering what she could. When our eyes met, I saw it instantly: the sharp glare of shame and embarrassment. Moments later, her head dropped. "Ma, do not worry about that," I said gently. "I have it." A heavy silence settled between us, lingering longer than either of us knew how to fill. I stepped closer to help her up into her recliner. As I bent down and reached for her arm, I felt her resist. She turned toward me, eyes fixed and unwavering, and said, "Let me do it." In that moment, frustration gave way to clarity. A quiet voice rose within me: the stroke had already taken away her independence. Suddenly, I understood. She was not just trying to clean up a mess. She was fighting to hold on to herself—to prove she was still capable, still present, and still whole.

As caregivers, we often take away independence while believing we are helping. Yes, it would have been faster for me—but at what cost to her dignity? Time and time again, I found myself stepping in when I saw my mother struggling to put on her shoes, button her coat, or lift a washcloth to her face. Each time, she would insist, "I can do it." Watching her struggle was painful. Letting go of my instinct to become her hands, feet—even her thoughts—required more strength than stepping in ever did. At first, I did not realize that in my efforts to make things easier, I was slowly stripping away her autonomy and asking her to move at my pace instead of honoring her own. There were moments when she would quietly watch me bring her food, especially when I began cutting it up without asking. Again, I had to learn how the smallest gestures—done without permission—could erode independence. One day she finally said, "You act as if I am not even here. You can at least let me try." What she was really saying was unmistakable: "I am not invisible. I am still here."

Caregiver Ree – My Greatest Lesson

My greatest lesson while taking care of my mother was completing the assignment God had given me. Approximately ten years ago, my mother was released from the hospital after suffering multiple pulmonary embolisms in her lungs. Although the doctor recommended rehab before coming home, my sister and I decided to take care of her at home. I moved in with my mother where I learned to be patient while taking care of her, assisting with her meals, cleaning the home, and taking care of financial matters. After a while, the family and my prayers were answered and my mother progressed to a state where she could manage on her own. Since she had always been an independent type person, I could sense she desired her privacy as much as possible I enrolled in school and volunteered one day a week at the hospital. Nonetheless, I felt that God was guiding me to recognize it was time for my departure. Although I was not aware of this, my daughter would need me.

Leaving my mother's, I became a caregiver to my daughter who unexpectedly became very ill. I thank God that I was in a position to take total care of her, and she was very appreciative for my support. After a number of years, my daughter was able to return to work. Now it was my time to live my life for me, or so I thought. Two years later, I was my mother's caregiver again after she fell and injured her hip and experienced other medical concerns. Although my sister and I tried caretakers coming into her home, it was not enough support. She needed around the clock care, so I left my job and moved back in with my mother temporarily. As my mother's health improved, I was able to move out while continuing to support her care with other additional help.

Well, I guess you might ask, "What was the lesson learned?" The answer to that is that God is still in control. Although I had different plans, my plans were in His Hand. I could not have taken on these responsibilities without God as my Helper. It was only God that gave me the strength to be a caregiver for my mother, then heal my mother so that I could leave and provide caregiving support to my daughter.

We may have our plans for our life, but I will never move forward with any plans without consulting my Lord and Savior. Lesson learned!!

Caregiver Patricia – Endless Love

About eight years ago, my life changed in a way I was not prepared for. I lost my mother to cancer—but what stays with me most is not only her passing, but the sacred six weeks that led up to it.

During that time, I became her primary caregiver in our home. My three children rearranged their work schedules and daily routines so they could be present—to support both their grandmother and me. Our home shifted into something different during those weeks. It became quieter. Slower. Holier.

What made it all so shocking was how suddenly it happened. My mother had not been sick or confined to a bed. She was diligent about her health and rarely missed a doctor's appointment. What began as a routine visit, with nothing more than standard blood work, turned into a phone call that altered everything. A few days later, her doctor called to tell me that my mother was terminally ill and had approximately six to eight weeks to live. I remember holding the phone and feeling as if I had stepped outside of my own body.

The words sounded unreal—like they belonged to someone else's life, not mine. Hospice was mentioned, and I could barely process what I was hearing. I kept thinking, How can this be true? How does a routine appointment turn into a goodbye?

Years before, my mother had entrusted me with more and more of her life. She had decided she no longer wanted to manage her business affairs or drive, and I had stepped into the role of caregiver without hesitation. Long before illness entered the picture, she had shared one very clear wish with me: if the time ever came for hospice care, she wanted to remain at home. Surrounded by family. In familiar spaces. At peace. And so, that is exactly what we did. I waited to share the full reality of her condition until the hospice care team could be present. When they arrived a day or two later, they met us with grace, patience, and compassion. They spoke gently with my mother, my daughter, and me, explaining their role and the process of dying in a way that was honest but deeply humane. Their presence felt like a covering—steady, respectful, and kind. Even then, I continued to pray for my mother's healing. Like so many believers, I held space for hope while also learning how to surrender. The hospice team walked with us every step of the way. No question went unanswered. No concern was dismissed. Their professionalism was matched only by their empathy.

They ministered not just to my mother's physical needs, but to our family's emotional and spiritual ones as well. Their care left an imprint on our hearts that will never fade. During those weeks, something profound happened between my mother and me. As I cared for her—managing medications, helping with hygiene, preparing the few foods and liquids she could tolerate—I felt our bond deepen in ways words cannot fully describe. Her appetite was small, and many times I gently encouraged her to eat or take a sip, knowing each moment mattered. Through it all, she never complained. Not once. Not about pain. Not about fear.

My mother loved God. She trusted His Word. When her eyesight failed and she could no longer read the Bible for herself, she would whisper to me and ask that I tell her the stories. I spoke Scripture into the quiet hours—day and night—sharing familiar passages, reminding her of God's promises. Even as her body weakened, her faith remained strong.

There were many moments when I cried alone. Moments of exhaustion. Moments when the weight of what was coming felt unbearable. But when I was with her, I tried to offer only love—gentle smiles, tender touch, whispered prayers for comfort, peace, and rest.

Six weeks after entering hospice care, my mother passed away peacefully. A dear family friend and I were with her when she took her final breath. There was no struggle. Just stillness. And grace.

Caregivers William and Dorothy

Compassionate Love and Commitment

William and I were in our early thirties when we first noticed that his mother was experiencing cognitive changes, including dementia-related confusion and delusions. She frequently called us accusing her husband of having another woman in his room. On several occasions, she contacted the police and asked them to come and remove him from the home. These incidents occurred so often that local law enforcement eventually began calling us directly to verify whether there was a legitimate need to respond.

As time progressed, William struggled with denial regarding his mother's declining health. That changed on a scorching July day when we were on our way to visit his parents. We took an alternate route and noticed a woman walking alone on a back road, wearing a hat in extreme heat. As we approached, we realized it was his mother. She had intended to walk to her sister's house but became disoriented and lost. We brought her home and helped cool her down. William's father had no idea she had deviated from her route or that she had become lost. That moment marked a turning point—William had to accept that his mother was ill and required supervision and care.

We decided it was time to bring her into our home. At the time, she was taking medication for type 2 diabetes and low-dose blood pressure. After moving in with us, her diet was carefully monitored, and she was eating properly; as a result, she was eventually taken off all medications. To ensure her safety, we moved our bedroom upstairs so she could occupy the downstairs rooms. We also changed door locks to prevent her from wandering out of the home.

While visiting her oldest son, she fell in his yard and broke her ankle. Although it healed, the prolonged immobility caused her brain to "forget" how to walk. From that point forward, she was transported to Day Care in a wheelchair. Later, while at the facility, she fell while attempting to transfer from a chair to a restroom stool, resulting in a broken hip that required surgical repair. This incident caused a significant setback. Although she returned briefly to Day Care, her decline accelerated, and she ultimately became unable to continue attending. At that time, in-home nursing care was initiated.

Our greatest reward was being able to provide a loving home for William's parents for ten years and to serve as their advocates in securing appropriate services and care. One of our greatest challenges was navigating the complex system and overcoming the numerous barriers required to access services, including Virginia's restrictive resource limits for eligibility.

We maintained our emotional, physical, and spiritual health through strong family support. We alternated church attendance for spiritual renewal and utilized respite care at nursing homes for brief periods. Our mutual love and support for one another sustained our commitment to caring for his parents.

William's mother passed away in July 2003, and his father followed in March 2004. His father remained mentally sharp until his passing and often served as our trusted source of feedback when others assisted with their care. When they both left us, we had peace in knowing we had done everything possible to keep them out of a nursing home and to provide them with dignity, love, and a quality life.

Both lived long enough to know their grandson and shared seven meaningful years with him. That, in itself, was a profound blessing.

Caring for my mother in her final days changed me forever. It taught me that caregiving is not only an act of service, it is an act of love, surrender, and sacred presence.

Reflective Moments for My Journal

Write your thoughts down in your *Reflective Journal*. Share them with someone you trust or say them aloud in prayer. Your voice deserves to be heard—even if only by you and God.

1. Caregivers wear many hats. From the three stories shared, what roles did each caregiver assume, and how did those roles impact them and their mothers?

2. At what point in the caregiving journey did you begin to feel unseen or invisible?

3. What steps, if any, did you take to practice self-care without allowing guilt to overshadow your well-being?

4. How has your faith, or spiritual grounding, sustained you during seasons of caregiving or loss?

5. How has caregiving changed your understanding of purpose and what it truly means to live a meaningful life in the season of aging?

CHAPTER 6

WE HAVE SOMETHING TO SAY

"Carry each other's burdens, and in this way you will fulfill the law of Christ,"
Galatians 6:2, NIV

The voices of older adults are too often overlooked in conversations that shape families, faith communities, healthcare systems, and public policy. *Vision in Visibility: The Silent Generation Speaks* offers a space for those voices to be heard—honestly, thoughtfully, and without apology. The following questions and responses reflect lived experiences of aging in a world that frequently values speed over wisdom and youth over longevity. They reveal moments of being unseen, the emotional weight of loneliness, the shifting roles within families, and the deep reliance on faith, resilience, and community. Together, these reflections illuminate not only the challenges of aging, but also the strength, insight, and enduring value of a generation that continues to contribute, teach, and love.

WHAT THE SILENT GENERATION IS SAYING

Questions	Key Responses
1. When was the first time you felt overlooked or unseen because of your age?	• At church — views were ignored or dismissed as "outdated." • Family and friends visited less over time. • Not invited out because of mobility, even though they wanted to go. • Government benefits don't reflect rising cost of living on fixed income.
2. How did it make you feel? How did you respond?	• Felt sad, deserted, unheard, discarded, and disrespected. • Withdrew, became quieter, and participated less in meetings and activities
3. What beliefs about aging may need to shift?	• Need to stop simply "being content" when things are not in your best interest. • Aging is a blessing, but learning must continue. • Need to learn more about technology to access services. • Need to ask more questions instead of settling. • Need to get out more instead of staying home except for church

4. How have your roles changed over time, and how has faith shaped aging?	• Once cared for children; now children help care for you. • Faith remains strong; trust in God through aging. • Aging is viewed as a blessing from God.
5. What dream feels "too late" but still calls to you?	• Better health habits (diet and exercise). • Continuing education for better income. • Learning to play piano. • Learning more about computers. • Traveling more.
6. Who needs to hear that they have value regardless of age?	• Senior friends. • Church friends and Senior Café community. • Your children — especially when they help physically and financially
7. How does loneliness affect older adults? How do you overcome it?	**Impact:** • Causes depression, confusion, and mental health struggles. • Creates feelings that "no one cares." **How you cope:** • Attend Senior Citizens Café and outings. • Go to church and trips when invited. • Call friends and family daily. • Serve as a listener and support to others.

8. What has your healthcare experience been like?	• Good plan, but transportation is often needed. • Medicare and drug premiums rising faster than Social Security increases. • Some doctors no longer accept certain plans, forcing changes.
9. What has your experience been as a caregiver?	• Requires compassion, patience, and understanding. • Must respect seniors' need for structure and timing. • Medicaid payments are often delayed. • Must keep careful records for the state. • Pay is often too low for the level of care required. • All people needing care deserve love, respect, safety, and dignity.
10. What legacy do you want to leave?	**As a caregiver:** • Love your neighbor as yourself. • Treat others as you want to be treated. • Help wherever you go. **As a senior:** • Be "better, not bitter." • Impact younger generations positively. • Be remembered as someone who made the world better. • "Model the way."

Taken together, these reflections remind us that aging is not a withdrawal from life, but a continued journey of growth, meaning, and contribution. The experiences shared here call for greater compassion, inclusion, and intentional listening—within families, churches, healthcare systems, and society as a whole. They challenge us to see older adults not as burdens or afterthoughts, but as bearers of wisdom, faith, and lived history. The legacy expressed through these responses is clear: to love generously, to remain engaged, to resist bitterness, and to leave the world better than it was found. In honoring these voices, we take an essential step toward making the invisible visible and ensuring that no generation is left unheard.

Write your thoughts down in your *Reflective Journal*. Share them with someone you trust or say them aloud in prayer. Your voice deserves to be heard —even if only by you and God.

I have something to say. What do you have to say?

Chapter 7

NEVER TOO LATE: BE A GOOD STEWARD OF YOUR HEALTH

"They will still bear fruit in old age, they will stay fresh and green,"
Psalm 92:14, NIV

What a blessing it is to greet each morning with a spirit of gratitude. Growing older is a gift from God. Many of us can say before our feet touch the floor, we whisper, "Thank You, Lord." This is not because everything feels perfect, but because you and I understand the gift of presence. We have learned over the years that taking care of our bodies matters. Unfortunately, in some cases, it may have been too late to prevent serious health challenges. We can believe that no matter where we may be in life's health challenges, there is still hope to live a better life. Being a good steward of our health is not vanity but responsibility. How we think about aging, about sickness, about how long we expect to live matters more than we were ever taught.

Our health journey is not to be taken alone. You and I need others to support us. Adopting a holistic approach to health care should be a priority for all individuals, especially older adults. Along life's way, we find that family, friends, neighbors, faith-based organizations, medical professionals, educators, and policy makers are all needed on our team. Author Jo Ann Jenkins in her book "Disrupt Aging," wrote that "Health is much more than the absence of illness; it is what gives us a sense of well-being and the vitality that allows us to experience life in a meaningful and satisfying way.... we need to maintain a vibrant lifestyle by accounting for our physical, mental, emotional, economic, social, and spiritual well-being."[10]

Yet, it is impossible to ignore the health care disparities in our society. Dr. Martin Luther King, Jr. in a press conference in Chicago before speaking to the Medical Committee for Human Rights on March 25, 1966, was quoted as saying, "Of all the forms of inequality, injustice in health is the most shocking and inhumane."[11] Too many of us live with the daily reality of healthcare inequality leading to a feeling of invisibility. This is a call for you and I to become our own advocate for quality health care and to stand collectively with others and with those organizations who are challenging the status quo to address health care disparities for us, the older adult.

We are seeing older adults taking responsibility for their personal health. This is a mindset change. Let us turn our attention to a quote that Satchel Paige, Hall of Fame legendary baseball pitcher asked, "How old would you be if you did not know how old you are?"[12] When he entered the major leagues, he had not seen his birth certificate and did not know his age. Yet he understood that it was not just about his chronological age, but that his mindset was key in his outstanding performance on the baseball field. He was not locked into the myth by society's standards that he was considered too old to be a professional baseball player, and an outstanding one at that. Neither should we be locked into a limited mindset of healthy aging as we grow older. So, ask yourself the question, "How old would you be if you did not know how old you are?" What prevents you from becoming a more active older adult? Today you and I are seeing more of this mindset as we make decisions on how we choose to age.

Now it is not realistic to expect every older adult to make this type of decision based on various challenges they may be facing in their lives. No two people are alike when we discuss health challenges, life circumstances, economic status, family support, or access to health care.

However, no matter where we are as older adults in our health journey, support is needed from all levels of society.

In 3 John 1:2, NKJV, God's word tells us that we are to prosper and be in health as our soul prospers. Let this scripture be a reminder that caring for the body is connected to caring for the soul. We find older women and men being more intentional about their health through various ways, including exercises, weightlifting, working out, pickle ball, marathons, and focusing on mental health, nutritional habits, and other community-based activities. As discipline and commitment take the lead, we are seeing mindsets change and overall health improvements contributing to being the best you can be at each season in your life. Moses was 80 years old when he was called by God to his ministry. It is not uncommon these days to see 70 plus year old women and men who are models, weightlifters, and marathon runners. Many actors on television and the movies started their career later in life.

Our lives are routine only if we decide to be guided by a routine lifestyle. Jesus spoke about putting new wine in old wineskins in Matthew 9:17, NIV. Encourage yourself and others as you give up the old habits and routines holding you hostage – the lack of exercising, eating unhealthily, and not getting enough rest are just a few. Be the prepared new wineskin Jesus spoke about to receive the new wine - a new way of thinking and acting so that the new wine can be poured into you as you walk in a new mindset and healthier lifestyle. Choose a scripture that speaks to your heart on stewarding your health and post it where it is easily visible to you for immediate encouragement.

Before concluding this chapter, there is a story that was shared with me during an interview on healthcare and its inequalities. The story below caught my attention as I recalled the quote from Dr. King on the inequalities of health care. Remember, just as Janet in the story below decided to see, we must choose to see and then make a difference through advocating for ourselves and others.

Janet's Story

About 10 years ago, I was part of a pre-med mission trip focused on the spiritual and mental wellness of patients in long-term hospitals and nursing homes. I expected to gain empathy – and I did – but what I encountered changed the way I viewed health injustice and aging. As part of the group, I listened, prayed, and asked patients how their lives and their faith had been affected by being there. Many were grateful to be seen and heard. But so many spoke of emptiness, loneliness, and spiritual depletion. One nursing home for older adults, located in a low-income community, was devastating. Entering the facility, my nose wrinkled at the stench. The facility was hot, dim, and riddled with flies. Residents spoke of depression, rarely receiving visitors, living quarters cramped spaces and shared with another resident. There was an overall feeling of hopelessness. It was devastating to witness the residents living in these conditions.

Write your thoughts down in your *Reflective Journal.* Share them with someone you trust or say them aloud in prayer. Your voice deserves to be heard—even if only by you and God.

1. What does it mean to me that I am still here? Who did not make it to this age that I carry with me? How often do I pause to thank God for the simple gift of another morning?

2. What gifts, callings, or dreams do I believe God placed in me that I have put on the shelf because of age, health, or fear? What might obedience look like for me now, in this season?

3. In what ways have I honored my body as a vessel God entrusted to me? In what ways have I neglected it—physically, emotionally, or spiritually? What is one small act of stewardship I can commit to without shame or comparison?

4. Recall a time I felt dismissed, rushed, or invisible—especially related to my health or aging. How did it affect my spirit?

5. What would advocating for myself look like, and who could stand with me when I need support?

Chapter 8

GENERATIONAL CONNECTIONS — HOLDING THE BRIDGE BETWEEN THEN, NOW, AND WHAT IS COMING

"One generation commends your works to another; they tell of your mighty acts."
Psalm 145:4, NIV

In my life experiences, I have learned this much to be true: God never meant for us to walk this life alone, and He surely did not intend for us to age out of relationship. Gray hair is not a dismissal notice. It is a calling card. It says we have lived long enough to remember, long enough to testify, and long enough to teach. From the beginning, God designed us for connection—family to family, generation to generation. Just as building a healthy body requires effort from many directions, so too does building a healthy legacy. It takes all of us—young and old, strong and weak, remembering and becoming—to link the past, the present, and the future together.

When we talk about intergenerational relationships, we must talk honestly about legacy. Folks often define legacy as property, money, or something written into a will after death. But I have come to know legacy as far more than material things. Legacy is what we pass on while we are still breathing. It is what is transmitted through our faith, our values, our stories, our habits, and our love. It is spiritual, relational, and yes, sometimes financial—but always intentional.

After my mother passed away in 2018, my children and I found something precious among her belongings: a handwritten note she had written five years earlier on my birthday. In that note, she gave God all the glory for family and for the blessing of gathering together on special occasions. She reminded us—no, she charged us—to always bless the Lord and to remain thankful for family. My mother was known for her cards. Birthday cards. Anniversary cards. "Just thinking about you" cards. She was the connector, the one who stitched us together with ink and Scripture and kind words. She was also the scribe—writing names, dates, prayers, and reminders so that no one would be forgotten.

When she went home to be with the Lord, the family began to ask, "Who's going to do it now?"

Who will write the cards?

Who will remember the dates?

Who will keep us connected?

That question still echoes with me, because it is the question every generation must answer.

Our generation must decide—on purpose—to become the bridge. We must commit ourselves to passing on family traditions, customs, heritage, and sound financial principles from one generation to the next. We must hand over not only what we owned, but what we learned.

We carry stories that cannot be Googled. We hold wisdom that only comes from endurance. We know what it means to trust God when the money was short, the door was closed, and the answer was delayed—but still on the way. At the same time, we need the younger generation just as much as they need us. We need their vision, their questions, their courage, and their understanding of a world that is changing faster than we ever imagined. Intergenerational connection is not about standing in front and pointing fingers; it is about walking alongside, listening as much as speaking.

I remember when the whole family gathered—parents, grandparents, aunts, uncles, cousins, and children into one house. The food was plenty, the laughter loud, and the stories rich. Those were the moments when family history was taught without a classroom. We learned who our people were. We heard about ancestors whose names we carried. We learned why certain traditions mattered and why some things were never done "because that is just not how our family moves."

Old photographs were passed around, bent at the corners, faded, sometimes torn. But through them, we saw ourselves. From those gatherings, legacy flowed naturally, like an inheritance of identity. That kind of passing down is a generational blessing. It feeds not only our children and grandchildren, but generations we may never live to see.

Over the years, I have listened to others share their family traditions, recipes passed down by feel instead of measurements; storytelling that taught history and faith; Sunday morning breakfasts before church with everyone around the table while parents and grandparents prayed.

Some families required their children to serve others before opening Christmas gifts, delivering presents to neighbors in need as a lesson in compassion. Others taught strong work ethics, business ownership, and financial independence—not through lectures, but through consistent examples, responsibility, and accountability. These lessons linger because they were lived.

About thirty years ago, I witnessed what I still call a miracle. In a small church, during the call to salvation, rededication and church membership, my husband who is deceased now did something none of us expected. He had lost his leg due to serious illness and relied on a cane to walk safely. Yet when the Spirit of the Lord moved upon his heart, he threw down that cane, stepped out into the aisle, and walked forward without assistance.

My pastor described what we witnessed as a miracle. Although today, he has been elevated to a Bishop in the Kingdom of God, he still speaks of that moment, reminding others how the Holy Spirit can move a believer beyond physical limitation and into divine obedience. For a moment, it was as if heaven met earth right there between the pews. My husband forgot what limited him because he remembered who led him. The Lord went before him, stood beside him, and surrounded him on every side.

That moment deposited something eternal into our family. His faith, his trust in God's Word, and his obedience to the Spirit left a spiritual legacy that continues to speak to generations after him. Faith lived out leaves footprints that time cannot erase.

These customs and practices often begin in families, but they stretch into communities, workplaces, and faith-based organizations. When Baby Boomers, Gen X, Millennials, Gen Z, and those coming behind them learn to walk together, we all grow stronger.

Our role is to mentor, encourage, and share, not always leading from the front, but supporting from beside. The experiences and spiritual strength that sustained us are not meant to die with us. As Psalm 71:18 declares: "Do not forsake me, my God, till I declare your power to the next generation, your mighty acts to all who are to come." At the same time, younger generations must be willing to listen, respect, and receive. Scripture reminds them in 1 Peter 5:5: "In the same way, you who are younger, submit yourselves to your elders..." When humility meets wisdom, everybody wins. If we do this well—if we honor one another, share openly, and walk together—our society will be better for it. We will prosper in the present and prepare faithfully for the future.

At this stage in our lives, we understand our assignment clearly: to remember, to testify, and to pass it on. We pray that when our time comes, someone will ask, "Who is going to do it now?"—and then rise up, pen in hand, faith in heart, ready to continue the story.

As we reflect in this season of our lives, we understand more clearly than ever that aging is not about fading away; it is about shining a guiding light. We are living witnesses, walking testimonies, and living letters read by those who come after us. What we choose to pass on—our faith, our stories, our love, and our obedience to God—will shape generations we may never meet on this side of heaven. May we remain willing vessels, committed to telling of the Lord's mighty acts, building bridges of connection, and leaving behind a legacy that points not to ourselves, but always to God. For one generation must indeed commend His works to another, until all who are to come know that the Lord has been faithful, then, now, and forevermore.

Write your thoughts down in your *Reflective Journal*. Share them with someone you trust or say them aloud in prayer. Your voice deserves to be heard—even if only by you and God.

1. What stories, traditions, or testimonies has God entrusted to me that I am responsible for passing on to the next generation?

2. In what ways has my life—through faith, obedience, or perseverance—left a spiritual imprint on my family or community?

3. Who were the “connectors” in my family or faith journey, and how am I being called to carry forward what they modeled for me?

4. How can I intentionally build bridges between generations—listening to younger voices while sharing the wisdom God has given me through experience?

5. What legacy am I actively creating today that will speak of God’s faithfulness long after I am gone?

CHAPTER 9

ADVOCACY AND SUPPORT: A BETTER WAY

"Trust in the Lord with all your heart and lean not on your own understanding; in all your ways submit to him, and he will make your paths straight."
Proverbs 3:5-6, NIV

You and I become representatives of change in our communities and the broader society when our voices are heard. Our voice is essential in decisions that affect our quality of life. In our communities, we need to feel safe. Our voices are important for advocating transportation, housing, health care, nutrition programs, and fighting ageism in our communities. Individually and collectively, we make a difference in the political, social, medical and civic decisions being made inside and outside our communities that directly impact us. That is what advocating for change is about.

Advocacy starts with everyday actions. By choosing not to endorse jokes that diminish the experience of aging, we help highlight the issue of ageism and acknowledge the importance of fostering change. It begins when we support organizations with a mission to end age discrimination. It begins when we mentor young men and women without judging them. It begins when we challenge the myth that growing older means becoming less.

True visibility is more than being seen or noticed as an older adult. It is being valued and respected for what the years have deposited in us through life experiences, wisdom gained, and much understanding. The changes begin with each of us.

Some of you are actively serving as agents of change. You have set an example. Keep supporting and encouraging neighbors, families, and other older adults who may not be involved. This responsibility is not just for older adults. We, along with others in society, have a responsibility to challenge the outdated belief that older adults have less to contribute or no voice just because of age.

When writing this chapter, I thought about an art exhibit I had seen several years ago focusing on layered perspectives. The chairs were of different heights. The structure featured three stacked chairs, held together by stilts which I labelled as societal values (ageism) and fastened with clasps. Like the silent generation may attest, eyes see something different now that years have passed. Reflecting on this today, I would designate the top chair representing older adults who are to be esteemed for their wisdom, experience, and commitment to faith and community. This chair's position is especially vulnerable because of ageism. The middle and bottom chairs represent younger generations, their knowledge, skills, experiences, connections with God and others, and those supporting change for older adults. This shows that we are all connected and need one another, regardless of age or the various roles we play. Should the clasps on the chairs, representing the different perspectives from generation to generation, be loosened or removed, the structural integrity of the chairs would diminish, leading to instability and potential collapse. Therefore, it is essential to integrate diverse perspectives and voices to collaboratively contribute to the advancement and reinforcement of our society. This approach will help recognize and uphold the value of older women and men for both present and future generations.

There is vision in visibility that transforms how we think, challenges outdated attitudes, and opens the door to a more meaningful way of living. It reflects you and me showing up fully in every stage of life—reclaiming a presence and a voice that may have quieted over time.

There is reason for hope as society begins to recognize older adults as valued contributors, with perceptions slowly evolving in spaces where we were once overlooked. Yet what matters most is this: **however, even with these strides, inequities persist**. We continue to encounter barriers in housing, workplaces, transportation, healthcare, retirement, and throughout society at large.

That reality calls for resilience—not just to endure, but to keep pushing forward. God promises us in Isaiah 46:4 (NLT) that " I will be your God throughout your lifetime...I made you, and I will care for you." Our hope must be active and enduring, grounded in the determination to create a more equitable world for ourselves and for the generations that follow. We must be that valuable catalyst for change so that when we look in the mirror, our presence is clear, recognized, and visible.

Write your thoughts down in your *Reflective Journal*. Share them with someone you trust or say them aloud in prayer. Your voice deserves to be heard—even if only by you and God.

1. Take the time to assess the impact of ageism in your life and others around you. How can you draw on your life experiences to become a change agent against ageism?

2. What organizations can you offer support to or join in the fight against age discrimination? Will you commit to becoming active if you are not already?

3. What are some specific actions you can take to overcome ageism in your family, community, and larger society?

4. Who or what helps you feel acknowledged and valued when you're feeling invisible or overlooked?

5. How will you become more involved with the younger generations to share the need for their support as advocates and to listen to their concerns?

CHAPTER 10

THRIVING WITH THE POWER OF GOD'S WORD

"So shall my word that goeth forth out of my mouth: it shall not return unto me void, but it shall accomplish that which it please..."

Isaiah 55:10-11, KJV

God is faithful! His purpose for our lives continues through every season, including our later years. Longevity does not mean the end of purpose or calling. Instead, it offers new opportunities to grow in faith, deepen our wisdom, and bless others. As we age God's Word remains our guide---offering strength, encouragement, and direction so that we may continue to bear fruit so that we may continue to bless generations to come.

God's Word brings peace in uncertain moments, rest in times of weariness, encouragement during challenges, and empowerment to keep moving forward. God's Word also brings healing, comfort, and renewed strength for the journey. Through the many experiences of life, most of us discover certain scriptures that become especially meaningful. These verses often stay with us, reminding us of God's faithfulness in both joyful and difficult seasons. Some of those passages may be found in the scriptures shared in this chapter. As you reflect on them and other beloved scriptures, may your prayers, meditation, and even your journaling deepen your appreciation for this season of life.

These scriptures highlight several important themes for this stage of life: the blessing of aging, the wisdom that comes with experience, the continuing purpose of older adults, the promise of renewed strength, and the calling to leave a legacy of faith. These passages remind us that God's work in and through us continues, and that every season of life can flourish when rooted in His Word.

AGING IS A BLESSING AND GIFT FROM GOD

1. Psalm 92:14 (NKJV) – "They will still bear fruit in old age; they will stay fresh and green."

2. Isaiah 46:4 (NIV) "Even to your old age and grey hairs I am he who will sustain you..."

3. Deuteronomy 31:8 (NIV) – "The Lord goes before you and will be with you; he will never leave you nor forsake you."

AGING BRINGS WISDOM

1. Job 12:12 (NIV) – "Is not wisdom found among the aged? Does not long life bring understanding?"

2. Proverbs 16:31 (NIV) – "Grey hair is a crown of glory; it is gained by living a godly life."

3. James 1:5 (NIV) – "If any of you lacks wisdom, you should ask God, who gives generously to all without finding fault, and it shall be given to you."

PURPOSE AND FRUITFUL

1. Matthew 6:33 (NKJV) – "But seek first the kingdom of God and His righteousness, and all these things shall be added to you."
2. Psalm 71:18 (NLT) – "Now that I am old and grey, do not abandon me, O God. Let me proclaim your power to this new generation ,..."
3. Psalm 92:12-14 (NLT) – "But the godly will flourish like palm trees...Even in old age they will still produce fruit; they will remain vital and green."

STRENGTH AND RENEWAL

1. Isaiah 40:31 (NLT) – "But those who trust in the Lord will find new strength..."
2. 2 Corinthians 4:16 (NIV) – ".... Though outwardly we are wasting away, yet inwardly we are being renewed day by day."
3. Philippians 4:13 (NLT) – "For I can do everything through Christ, who gives me strength."

LEGACY AND GOD'S FAITHFULNESS

1. Psalm 143:10 (CEB) - "Teach me to do what pleases you, because you are my God. Guide me by your good spirit into good land."

2. Deuteronomy 32:7 (NIV) – "Remember the days of old; consider the generations long past."

3. Corinthians 3:18 (NKJV) – "But we all, with unveiled face, beholding as in a mirror the glory of the Lord, are being transformed into the same image from glory to glory, just as by the Spirit of the Lord."

Be transformed! Society's perception---reflections in the mirror--of aging women and men are evolving and will continue to do so—across all generations—as we commit to being a catalyst for change. And remember, change begins with each of us.

Invisibility no more!

Thank you for staying with me until the end of this journey!

VISION IN VISIBILITY RESOURCES

AARP

Nonprofit, Nonpartisan organization that empowers people to change how they live as they age.

Telephone: 1-888-687-2277

Online: AARP.org

VICAP (Virginia Insurance Counseling and Assistance Program)

Offers free Medicare counseling. Contact your local Area Agency on Aging.

Online: dars.virginia.org and follow steps for your local area.

NATIONAL INSTITUTE ON AGING (NIA)

Offers health and wellness information and ways to combat social isolation and loneliness.

Online: nia.nih.gov

VIRGINIA DEPARTMENT FOR AGING AND REHABILIITATIVE SERVICES

Telephone: (804) 662-7000

Online: dars.virginia.gov

This agency assists with independent living and dignity maintaining for older adults in Virginia. Below is one example of such an agency for those living in Southeastern Virginia. When using this site, locate your living area for information.

SENIOR SERVICES OF SOUTHEASTERN VIRGINIA

Telephone: (757) 461-9481 Online: ssseva.org

–Nonprofit organization supporting older adults and their caregivers through meals, transportation, community activities, in-home support, wellness classes, and more resources.

CAREGIVER ACTION NETWORK

Telephone: (Help Desk) 855-227-3640

Online: info@caregiveraction.org

This organization provides support services to caregivers.

ENDNOTES

1 Becky Levy, "Combating Ageism with Science: Robert Butler's Shaping of the National Institute on Aging" The Gerontonolist, Volume 65, Issue 2, February 2025, gnae 167, https://doi.org/10.1093/geront/gnae167

2 Jo Ann Jenkins, Disrupt Aging (New York: Public Affairs, 2016), p. 30

3 Jeanette Leardi, "Aging Sideways: Changing Our Perspectives on Getting Older" (2024)

4 Jo Ann Jenkins, Disrupt Aging (New York: Public Affairs, 2016), 40

5 National Institute on Aging Blog "Don't call me "old": Avoiding ageism when writing about aging, December 27, 2003, by Stephanie Morrison, Office of Communications and Public Liaison

6 Vivek Murphy, U.S. Surgeon General 2023

7 "Beyond the Hype with Alfred Edmund Jr. and MIT's Dr. Joseph Coughlin Presented in partnership with Manulife/John Hancock "Money Moves that Matter" Series Unpacking

Longevity Preparedness, Dr. Joe Coughlin, Director and Founder of Massachusetts Institute of Technology Age Lab-1

8 Article "Honoring Rosalynn Carter's Legacy by Prioritizing Caregivers" by Dr. Jennifer

Olsen, CEO, Rosalynn Carter Institute for Caregiving, posted on January 4, 2024 by Office of Disease Prevention and Health Promotion

9 2025 Edition of Caregiving in the US, by AARP and The National Alliance for Caregiving: published July 24, 2025

10 Jenkins, Disrupt Aging, 77

11 Martin Luther King Jr, Speech, Second National Convention of the Medical Committee for Human Rights, Chicago, March 25, 1966

12 Satchel Paige Biography.com

ABOUT THE AUTHOR

Patricia Terrangi retired after thirty years of service, twenty-five years working with the Virginia Department of Corrections and five with the federal government. She entered corrections in the administrative support field, and retired as a Senior Corrections Warden. During her career in corrections, she worked at seven different facilities, both male and female, and one year in the state of Maryland. Following her retirement in 2009, she immediately accepted a position as the Executive Director of Ministry Programs with the Mount Lebanon Missionary Baptist Church, affectionately known at that time as the Mount in Chesapeake, Virginia. She was employed in that position for three years until she decided it was time to spend more time with family and enjoying retirement to the fullest. She has been a partner at the Mount for over twenty-five years where she has faithfully served in various ministries and leadership roles. Currently, Patricia serves on the Council of Elders at the now Mount Global Fellowship of Churches under the leadership and direction of Bishop Kim W. and Dr. Elder Valerie K. Brown. She has served as an Assistant Director of the Ministers Training Program, and has volunteered her support to the online New Partners Ministry when she lived in a different state.

Patricia Terrangi's career is part of the legacy of leadership, service, and unwavering excellence across government, corrections, education, and faith-based organizations. She is a proud graduate of Bennett College in Greensboro, NC, and pursued ongoing academic work at the Virginia Commonwealth University. Her life's work stands as a compelling example of how experience deepens with age —and how one's most meaningful contributions often span decades, not chapters.

Patricia Terrangi values family time with her children, grandchildren and great-grandchildren. She currently resides in Virginia.

Connect with Patricia at Patricia@patriciaterrangi.com

www.ingramcontent.com/pod-product-compliance
Lightning Source LLC
LaVergne TN
LVHW010940110826
845149LV00013B/2690

* 9 7 9 8 9 9 3 2 1 4 5 3 5 *